Rookie
Read-About®
Geography

South America

High Point Media Center

by Rebecca Hirsch

Content Consultant
J. Miguel Kanai
University of Miami, Department of Geography

Reading Consultant
Jeanne Clidas
Reading Specialist

Children's Press®
An Imprint of Scholastic Inc.
New York • Toronto • London • Auckland • Sydney • Mexico City
New Delhi • Hong Kong • Danbury, Connecticut

Library of Congress Cataloging-in-Publication Data
Hirsch, Rebecca E.
  South America / by Rebecca Hirsch.
      p. cm. – (Rookie read-about geography)
  Includes index.
  ISBN 978-0-531-28981-5 (lib.bdg.) – ISBN 978-0-531-29281-5
(pbk.)
  1. South America–Juvenile literature. 2. South
America–Geography–Juvenile literature. I. Title.

  F2208.5.H57 2012
  980–dc23

                              2012013407

SCHOLASTIC, CHILDREN'S PRESS, ROOKIE READ-ABOUT®,
and associated logos are trademarks and/or registered trademarks of
Scholastic Inc.

1 2 3 4 5 6 7 8 9 10 R 22 21 20 19 18 17 16 15 14 13

Photographs © 2013: age fotostock: 22 (Charles Mahaux), 29, 31 top
left (Heeb Christian), 10 (Picture Contact BV), cover (Siegfried Kuttig);
Alamy Images/Juniors Bildarchiv: 20; AP Images/Andre Penner: 24, 31
bottom right; Getty Images/Francois Ancellet/Gamma-Rapho: 8; Media
Bakery/Adalberto Rios Szalay/Sexto Sol): 26; Shutterstock, Inc.: 30 (Karen
Givens), 16, 31 bottom left (Karim Wassmer), 4 (Ladynin); Superstock,
Inc.: 14, 31 top right (Axiom Photographic Limited), 12 (Michele Burgess),
18 (Wolfgang Kaehler).

Map by Matt Kania/www.maphero.com

Table of Contents

4   The Iguassu Falls in South America

Welcome to South America!

South America is a continent. It has 12 countries.

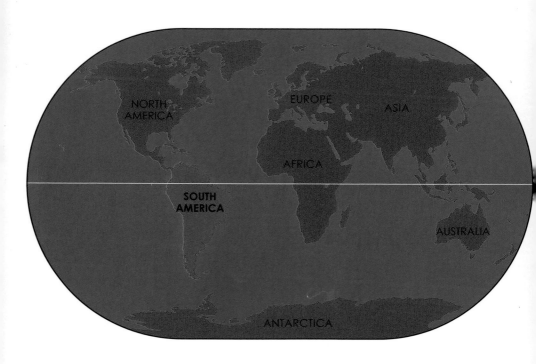

NORTH
AMERICA

EUROPE

ASIA

AFRICA

SOUTH
AMERICA

AUSTRALIA

ANTARCTICA

6

The largest pieces of land on Earth are continents. There are seven. South America is the **yellow** continent on this map.

A woman cuts plants in the Amazon rainforest.

People and Places

The Amazon Rainforest in South America is the biggest in the world. People use the plants for food and medicine.

Xingu Indian boys are good hunters.

Native people live in
the rainforest. They hunt,
fish, and farm together.

Children with a llama in Peru

The Andes Mountains are in South America. Llamas help people carry things up and down the mountains.

14   The Atacama Desert in Chile
has cracked mud.

South America has deserts. They are hot and dry. Some of the driest places on Earth are in South America.

A howler monkey

Amazing Animals

The rainforest is home to many animals. Monkeys live in the trees.

Scarlet macaws live in pairs.

Parrots live in the trees, too. They eat fruit and seeds.

Pink dolphins can be found
in South America.

Pink dolphins swim in the rainforest rivers. They catch fish with their long snouts.

Machu Picchu is in Peru.

Visit South America

Many people visit South America. They come to see where people lived long ago.

24

The Amazon River is the
second-longest river in the world.

They ride boats through the rainforest on the long Amazon River.

Sao Paulo, Brazil, is a busy city in South America.

They come to see South America's busy cities. Would you like to visit South America someday?

Modern Marvels

- The Itaipu Dam is on a river in South America.

- Workers moved the river to build the dam. They moved a lot of dirt and rock!

- The dam uses flowing water to make electricity.

- People in towns and cities use the electricity.

Try It!

What does the dam use to make electricity? What do cities and towns use electricity for? How do you use electricity?

28

Meet a Jaguar

- Jaguars are big cats.

- They live in the rainforests of South America.

- Jaguars are good swimmers. They love to play in the water.

- Mother jaguars teach their cubs how to hunt.

Words You Know

dam

desert

monkey

river

31

Index

Facts for Now

Visit this Scholastic Web site for more information
on South America:
www.factsfornow.scholastic.com
Enter the keywords **South America**

About the Author

Rebecca Hirsch is a scientist-turned-writer and the
author of many books for young readers.